# Hurricane!

## by Cynthia Pratt Nicolson

ANDREW WAS HERE

**Kids Can Press**

## For my wonderful kids, Sara, Ian and Vanessa

**Acknowledgments**
Many thanks to Dr. Lionel Pandolfo of the University of British Columbia for his comments on the draft manuscript of this book. Any errors that may have crept into the final book are my responsibility. Every book is a team effort, and I would like to thank all the staff at Kids Can Press for their cheerful, dedicated work on this series. I'm particularly grateful for the careful editing of Stacey Roderick and Val Wyatt, Patricia Buckley's persistent photo research, Bill Slavin's amusing illustrations and Julia Naimska's lively design.

Kids Can Press acknowledges the financial support of the Ontario Arts Council, the Canada Council for the Arts and the Government of Canada, through the BPIDP, for our publishing activity.

Published in Canada by          Published in the U.S. by
Kids Can Press Ltd.             Kids Can Press Ltd.
29 Birch Avenue                 2250 Military Road
Toronto, ON  M4V 1E2            Tonawanda, NY  14150

www.kidscanpress.com

Edited by Stacey Roderick and Val Wyatt
Designed by Julia Naimska
Printed and bound in Hong Kong, China, by Book Art Inc., Toronto

The hardcover edition of this book is smyth sewn casebound.
The paperback edition of this book is limp sewn with a drawn-on cover.

CM 02  0 9 8 7 6 5 4 3 2 1
CM PA 02  0 9 8 7 6 5 4 3 2 1

**National Library of Canada Cataloguing in Publication Data**

Nicolson, Cynthia Pratt
   Hurricane!

(Disaster)
Includes index.

ISBN 1-55074-906-4 (bound)   ISBN 1-55074-970-6 (pbk.)

1. Hurricanes — Juvenile literature.  I. Title.  II. Series: Disaster (Toronto, Ont.).

QC944.2.N53 2002        j551.55'2        C2001-904170-5

Kids Can Press is a *corus*™ Entertainment company

# CONTENTS

# HURRICANE
# Hammers Coast!

"Hurricane's coming!" weather experts warned North and South Carolina residents on September 21, 1989. For those living near the coast, it was time to get out. Fast!

Frantic families boarded up windows and threw what they could into their cars. Traffic

This satellite photo was taken just 10 hours before Hurricane Hugo struck North Carolina and South Carolina with violent winds, heavy rains and the highest surge of ocean flooding ever recorded on the east coast of the United States.

jammed the highways leading from the coast. But many people could not — or would not — leave. One group of

400 in McClellanville, South Carolina, crowded into a school cafeteria. Here they hoped to stay safe and dry.

Sea water floods the shore as Hurricane Hugo smashes into the Virgin Islands before veering northward. Hugo started as a mass of clouds near West Africa, then gathered speed and size as it swirled across the Atlantic Ocean. It ravaged Guadeloupe, Antigua, Puerto Rico and the Virgin Islands before heading for the mainland United States.

Around midnight, Hurricane Hugo hit land. The storm raged in the darkness, tearing down trees and telephone poles. It whipped roofs off houses and tossed them into the air. As it headed farther inland, Hugo knocked out power and dumped rain in a path 240 km (150 mi.) wide.

The advancing hurricane pushed a huge bulge of sea water, called a storm surge, onto the shore. In McClellanville, the water level rose 5 m (16 ft.) in just a few minutes. People in the dark cafeteria scrambled onto tables and lifted young children to keep their heads above water. Hours passed as the group stood trapped in the chest-high water, listening to the hurricane's groaning winds.

A little girl gets a comforting hug in a temporary shelter set up for victims of Hurricane Hugo. Thousands fled their homes to escape the hurricane's wild rampage.

Finally, in the early morning, the water level began to drop. In McClellanville, weary survivors climbed down from tables. Everyone there had survived the night. Elsewhere, people were not so lucky.

# HUGO HITS HARD

Hurricane Hugo was one of the worst storms ever to hit North America. It killed eighty-two people and caused enormous property damage. When survivors returned to their homes after Hugo's attack, they were shocked by the mess. Some neighborhoods looked as though they had been bombed.

**Firefighters inspect a collapsed house in Charleston, South Carolina, after Hurricane Hugo's attack. The giant storm killed dozens of people and destroyed property valued at over $7 billion.**

**A family gathers beside their destroyed home on the Caribbean island of Guadeloupe. As well as tearing down houses, Hugo ruined the island's banana and coffee crops and toppled its airport control tower.**

Hugo had smashed signs, electrical wires, fences and telephone poles. Its winds, which reached 208 km/h (130 m.p.h.), had stripped houses of their doors, roofs and chimneys and yanked tall trees out by their roots. Surging waters had plucked boats from coastal marinas and stranded them far from the shore.

Chainsaws whined as residents chopped up debris for burning or hauling away. Although the hurricane lasted only twelve days from start to finish, its destruction took months to repair. For the families of the people who died in the storm, life after Hugo was never the same.

# DISASTER DATA

Hurricane, cyclone and typhoon are different names for the same thing: a vast, spinning storm with winds over 119 km/h (74 m.p.h.) The word hurricane comes from Hunraken, the Mayan storm god of Central America. In the China Sea such a storm is called a typhoon, from the Chinese words *tai fung*, meaning "big wind." In the southwest Pacific Ocean and the Indian Ocean, it's known as a cyclone, from the Greek word for "coiled snake."

Splintered trees in South Carolina's Francis Marion National Forest show the power of Hurricane Hugo's high winds. The storm chewed up vast stretches of forest and destroyed enough lumber to build about 300 000 houses. For days after Hugo's rampage, the scent of pine filled the air.

# Birth of a HURRICANE

You won't find a hurricane forming in cold regions or in the middle of a continent. In fact, most places don't have the right conditions for a hurricane. What does it take? Warm water and moist air, plus some "spin" from Earth's rotation, are needed to produce the huge storms of spiraling winds that we call hurricanes.

Hurricanes are born over tropical oceans, where the water is very warm. Ocean temperatures must be over 27°C (80°F) for a hurricane to form. And the warm water must be deep — at least 60 m (about 200 ft.). (A thin layer of warm water won't do because a storm would mix it with the cold waters below.)

The warm water heats the air above it, and the air starts to rise. Water vapor in this rising, moist air cools and condenses to produce billowing clouds and thunderstorms.

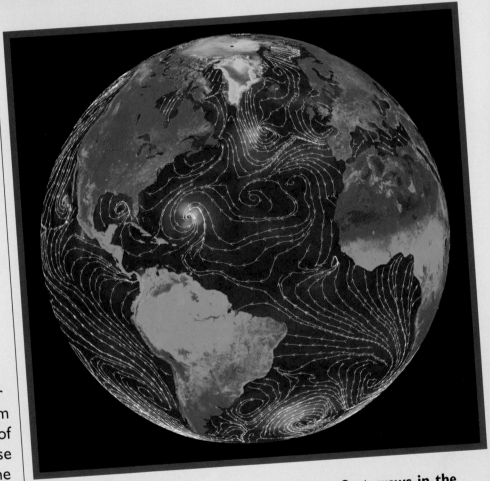

The rising air also leaves an area, or center, where the pushing force, or pressure, of the air is very low. Air from surrounding areas flows into this low-pressure center, creating strong winds. (You can feel wind blow from a high- to a low-pressure area when air escapes from a balloon.)

Hurricane Gert grows in the Atlantic Ocean off the east coast of Florida. Notice how the winds swerve as a result of Earth's rotation. Orange indicates the highest wind speeds.

The winds rush into the low-pressure center from every direction. But because of the effects of Earth's rotation, they swerve and start to spiral around the center. Meanwhile, as more air rises and cools, water vapor condenses to add heat energy to the storm.

The result is a spiraling storm of winds, clouds and rain. When the winds reach 119 km/h (74 m.p.h.) the storm is classified as a hurricane. In the Northern Hemisphere, hurricane winds spiral counterclockwise. In the Southern Hemisphere, hurricanes spin clockwise.

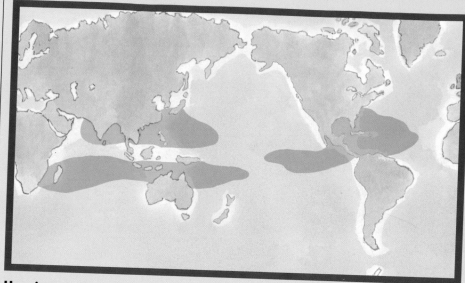

Hurricanes are born in the green tropical regions shown on this map. These areas have the warmth, moisture and swirling winds that hurricanes need.

**Children in West Palm Beach, Florida, use plastic garbage bags to sail on the winds of Tropical Storm Gordon in September 2000. The day before, Gordon's winds had reached hurricane speed.**

## You Try It

Differences in air pressure create a hurricane's strong winds. You can observe the amazing power of such differences with this experiment. You'll need 2 empty soda cans and 20 plastic drinking straws.

Lay 19 straws on a table so that they are close together but not touching. Stand the soda cans on the straws about 10 cm (4 in.) apart.

Hold the remaining straw so that it points toward one of the cans, on the side facing the other can. Now blow strongly and steadily through the straw. You are creating an area of low pressure next to the can. Watch as the higher pressure on the other side of the can pushes it into this low-pressure region. Can you make the two cans collide?

# Anatomy of a HURRICANE

A full-fledged hurricane is shaped like a huge doughnut, but it's far from being a motionless lump. Instead, a hurricane (shown in this cross-section) is an action-packed system of clouds, wind and rain.

A towering band of wind-whipped clouds surrounds the hurricane's eye. This ring, called the eye wall, is where the hurricane's winds are strongest. They spiral upward toward the top of the hurricane.

The hole in the middle of a hurricane is called its eye. Air in the eye is surprisingly calm, and the sky overhead is blue. A hurricane's eye can measure from 10 km to 50 km (6 mi. to 31 mi.) across.

In the very middle of the eye, cooler air sinks down. It becomes compressed and heated as it falls, absorbing water vapor on its way down. The result of this evaporation is a clear tunnel from the top of the hurricane down to the ocean's surface, a distance of about 15 km (9 mi.).

Spiraling winds flow toward the hurricane's low-pressure center.

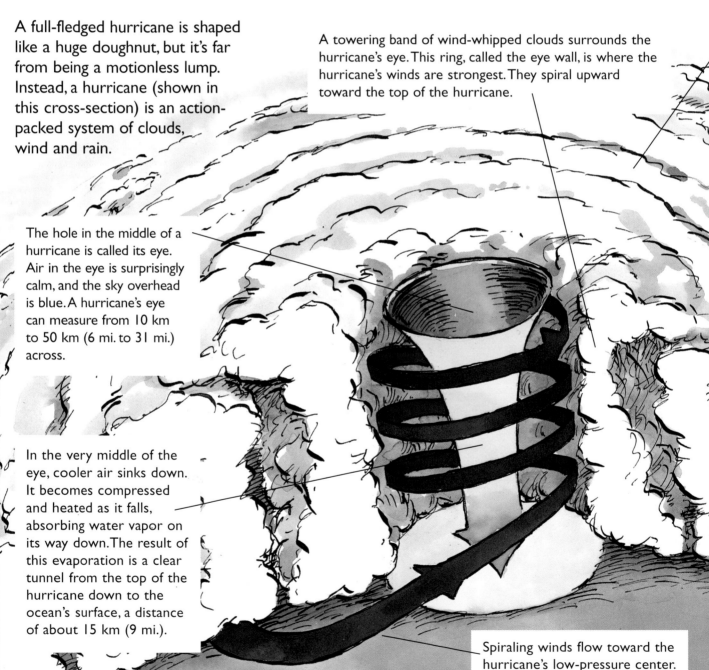

Surrounding the eye wall are lines of clouds called rain bands or cloud streets. These thunderstorm clouds are loaded with moisture, which falls as heavy rain. These clouds also swirl around the hurricane's eye but not as quickly as the eye wall.

At its outer edges, the hurricane weakens. Here the clouds lighten and winds become less forceful. Still, even the rim of a hurricane can bring destructive winds and pounding rain.

# DISASTER DATA

What's the difference between hurricanes and tornadoes? Plenty! Most hurricanes last several days; tornadoes last only minutes. Hurricanes are much bigger than tornadoes — on average about 2000 times greater across. Think of it this way: if a tornado were as wide as a hamburger, a hurricane would be the length of an entire football stadium.

Although much smaller than hurricanes, tornadoes have more intense winds. The fastest recorded hurricane wind speed is 240 km/h (150 m.p.h.). Tornado winds can be twice as fast: up to 480 km/h (300 m.p.h.).

Here's an added twist. Strange as it seems, tornadoes often form *inside* hurricanes. This happens when a hurricane reaches land, creating the turbulent air conditions that are just right for tornadoes.

Almost all hurricanes that strike North America produce at least one tornado. In 1992, Hurricane Andrew spawned 62 tornadoes. In 1967, Hurricane Beulah gave birth to a whopping 141 tornadoes.

A tornado touches down near Dimmitt, Texas, on June 2, 1995. While hurricanes form over oceans, tornadoes usually form over dry land.

# Deadly Diary: HURRICANE FLOYD

In the steamy days of the late summer of 1999, a wave of stormy weather drifted away from the west coast of Africa. Storm clouds gathered, forming a center of low pressure. Winds rushed in from high-pressure areas around the center. Hurricane Floyd was being born.

**September 8: The growing storm begins to spin as it drifts west across the Atlantic Ocean.**

**September 9: Winds reach speeds of 63 km/h (39 m.p.h.), making this an official tropical storm.**

**September 12: Winds exceed 119 km/h (74 m.p.h.). Tropical Storm Floyd becomes a full-fledged hurricane.**

September 14: Weather officials post warnings as Floyd ravages parts of the Bahamas and threatens the United States.

September 15: Hurricane Floyd drifts north, just missing Florida and Georgia.

September 16: Hurricane Floyd hits North Carolina. Heavy rain causes massive flooding. About 69 people are killed.

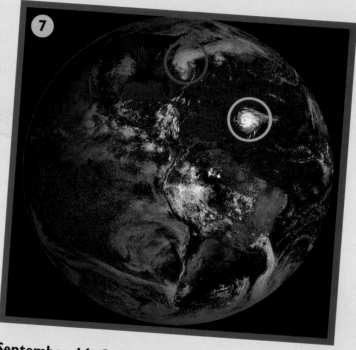

September 16: Cooler temperatures and a lack of moisture weaken Hurricane Floyd (red circle), as it moves northward. Soon it will completely disappear. Meanwhile, a new storm (yellow circle) is swirling in the Atlantic. Hurricane Gert is on its way.

This map shows the path of Hurricane Floyd in early September 1999. Numbers show Floyd's location when each satellite photo was taken.

"The storm's not over! We're in the lull! Get back to safety!" yelled weather officer Richard Gray, running onto the street to warn Miami residents on the morning of September 18, 1926. Throughout the night, powerful winds and rain had pummeled their city. Now, with clear skies overhead, many thought the danger was past. They raced outside in celebration, not realizing that they were in the eye of the hurricane. Within forty-five minutes, they would be struck by the deadly winds of the back half of the storm.

When a hurricane's eye is directly overhead, the storm's strong winds and heavy rainfall stop. Suddenly, skies are clear and the air is calm. Many people go outside because they think the storm is over. They can be injured or killed when the second half of the hurricane strikes with full force.

# Inside THE EYE

From inside a hurricane, the eye wall rises steeply. Directly overhead, a disk of clear sky contrasts with the storm's heavy, swirling clouds. Birds are sometimes caught in a "cage" formed by a hurricane's eye wall.

Hurricane Fefa's eye opens over the Pacific Ocean in this photo taken from above. Fefa was a strong hurricane that did no damage because it did not hit land.

A hurricane's doughnut shape is caused by balanced forces. The tendency of the spinning winds to move away from the center of the storm is balanced by the low air pressure that pulls them in. The result? The clouds of the eye wall stay in position, and the eye is formed.

As a hurricane becomes more powerful, its eye shrinks. The air pressure in its center drops lower and lower, and the winds in the eye wall blow faster. When the storm weakens and the air pressure rises, winds begin to slow and the eye expands.

A fierce hurricane lashes the Miami beachfront on September 18, 1926. Many people rushed outside into the storm's calm eye, only to be killed when the second half of the hurricane arrived. In all, the storm took 240 lives and left 18 000 people homeless.

## YOU TRY IT

A hurricane's eye forms when the straight-ahead motion of the spinning winds is balanced by inward pull created by low air pressure. You can see a similar effect with a pail of water. (This activity must be done outdoors!) Pour water into a small beach pail until it is half full. Stand in an open space, well away from other people. Hold the pail with one hand and swing it quickly in large circles.

What happens? If you are swinging fast enough, the water stays in the pail, even when the pail is upside down. The force of your swinging is balanced by the pull of your arm on the pail.

Just as water in the pail stays on its circular path, the clouds in a hurricane's eye wall circle around its clear center. Balanced forces keep both the pail water and eye wall clouds in place.

# Measuring THE POWER

All hurricanes are powerful, but some are much stronger than others. To measure a hurricane's strength, or intensity, meteorologists use the Saffir-Simpson hurricane intensity scale. This scale has five levels based on wind speed, surface air pressure and height of storm surges. The actual destruction caused by a hurricane depends on where and when it hits and how much warning has been given for people to prepare.

**Category 1** hurricanes are called "minimal." Their winds range from 119 km/h to 153 km/h (74 m.p.h. to 95 m.p.h.). These hurricanes damage trees and shrubs and may flood low-lying roads near the coast. Hurricane Earl, which flooded parts of the Florida Panhandle in 1998, was a category 1 hurricane.

**Category 2** storms are "moderate." Their winds range from 154 km/h to 177 km/h (96 m.p.h. to 110 m.p.h.). They can blow down trees and damage roofs, doors and windows. People living on the shoreline may have to evacuate when a category 2 hurricane is on the way. Hurricane Georges, in 1998, was ranked as category 2. It struck the northern Caribbean islands, including Haiti, killing over 500 people and destroying thousands of homes.

**Category 3** hurricanes are "extensive." Along with categories 4 and 5, these storms are called "major" hurricanes. With winds from 178 km/h to 208 km/h (111 m.p.h. to 129 m.p.h.), they can destroy mobile homes and cause serious flooding in coastal areas. Hurricane Fran, in 1996, was a category 3 storm. It hit North Carolina, Virginia Maryland, and killing thirty-seven people.

**Cyclone Tracy** howled through Darwin, Australia, for four hours on December 25, 1974. Tracy, a category 4 cyclone, had winds reaching speeds of 240 km/h (150 m.p.h.) and destroyed 8000 homes.

**Category 4** hurricanes are "extreme," with winds from 209 km/h to 248 km/h (130 m.p.h. to 154 m.p.h.). They can completely destroy roofs, windows and doors and flood inland as far as 10 km (6 mi.). Hurricane Andrew, in 1992, was a category 4 hurricane.

**Category 5** hurricanes are called "catastrophic." These are the strongest hurricanes known, with winds of more than 248 km/h (154 m.p.h.). They blow down signs, trees and roofs and completely overturn small buildings. People up to 16 km (10 mi.) from the shore may need to evacuate their homes. Hurricane Camille, in 1969, was a category 5 hurricane (see page 18).

# DISASTER DATA

Although hurricanes cause terrible damage, they also help us in a surprising way. They are an important part of Earth's complicated weather system. Like giant fans, storms take hot air from the tropics and move it toward the poles. They help balance temperatures and moisture around the Earth. Without hurricanes and other storms, vast areas of our planet would be too hot for animal and human life.

Most Atlantic hurricanes intensify slowly. They remain at category 1 or 2 until they drift northward and disappear. Major hurricanes (categories 3, 4 and 5), on the other hand, change rapidly from weak to strong. This strengthening often happens in just one or two days and can take forecasters by surprise.

While the forces that cause such growth in hurricane strength aren't completely understood, scientists believe they depend to some extent on the warmth of the ocean water that a hurricane passes over.

A sailboat lies stranded on a Miami highway after Hurricane Andrew devastated Florida in August 1992. The boat was swept inland by a storm surge (bulge of ocean water) caused by the category 4 hurricane.

# Surges of DESTRUCTION

Hurricanes are known for high winds and heavy rains. But danger comes from the sea as well as the sky. Storm surges — huge swells of ocean water along the shoreline caused by hurricanes — have claimed thousands of victims.

surge

Storm surges happen when a hurricane's winds push the ocean surface ahead of the storm. A dome of water forms that can be 160 km (100 mi.) wide and can raise water levels at the shore by 6 m (20 ft.) or more.

The size of a surge depends on the shape of the shoreline, the speed of the hurricane winds and the angle at which the hurricane hits land. The largest storm surge on record happened in Bathurst Bay, Australia, in 1899. Water in the bay rose 13 m (about 43 ft.) above normal sea level.

When a storm surge hits during high tide, the effects can be deadly. The hurricane's winds stir up choppy waves and raise already high water to extreme levels. People trapped in houses or cars along the coast have no way of escaping from the surging water.

A 6 m (20 ft.) storm surge from Hurricane Camille flooded Pass Christian, Mississippi, in August 1969. The surge obliterated the Richelieu Apartments, shown here before and after Camille. A group of 32 people had ignored evacuation warnings and stayed for a "hurricane party" in the building. All but two of them were drowned. One woman survived by clinging to debris. She was later found in the branches of a tree.

Huge waves from Hurricane Carol crash into beachfront homes in Connecticut in August 1954. The hurricane's storm surge destroyed hundreds of summer cottages and homes.

Storm surges have been especially deadly in Bangladesh, a small country near India. Low-lying land and the narrow Bay of Bengal make rising water particularly dangerous there. In 1970, close to 500 000 people died when a tropical cyclone hit the area.

A man and his sons wade across a flooded highway in the state of Orissa in eastern India. A tropical cyclone (hurricane) hit the area in October 1999 with a storm surge that left millions homeless. Officials estimate that 10 000 people died.

## YOU TRY IT

Has your name been attached to a hurricane? You can find out by checking the hurricane names at this Web site: **www.nhc.noaa.gov/aboutnames.html**

From 1953 to 1979, the U.S. Weather Bureau gave women's names to hurricanes in the Atlantic Ocean. When women complained, men's names began to be used as well. Now Atlantic hurricanes are named according to alphabetical lists that alternate men's and women's names.

Typhoons in the northwest Pacific are rarely given human names. Most are named after flowers, animals, trees or even foods from different Asian countries.

# A KILLER STRIKES

What do you get when you combine a major hurricane with a collapsing volcano? Incredible disaster!

Most hurricanes pass by in a few hours. Not Hurricane Mitch. The massive storm hung over Central America for several days in late October 1998. It pelted Honduras, Nicaragua, El Salvador and Guatemala with heavy rain. Some spots reported over 122 cm (48 in.) of rain in just six days.

Rivers and lakes flooded their banks. Roads were washed out and bridges destroyed. People were forced to climb onto rooftops to escape the rising waters. Many parents tied their children to the branches of tall trees to keep them from drowning. About 400 crocodiles escaped from a science institute, adding to the danger.

Hurricane Mitch hovers over Central America, heavy with moisture gathered from both the Caribbean Sea and the Pacific Ocean. Mitch dumped the moisture as rain, flooding the region and destroying thousands of homes.

With umbrellas raised against the relentless rain, Honduran residents watch the overflowing Choluteca River. Their country was devastated by Hurricane Mitch in October 1998.

The mountains of Honduras and Nicaragua seemed to squeeze even more water from the hurricane. On top of the Casita volcano, an old crater filled with water. When the pressure of the water became too great, the crater walls collapsed, releasing a deadly mudslide. It rushed down the mountainside, sweeping away nearby villages and towns. About 2000 people were buried in the torrent of mud.

A young girl is airlifted to safety by a rescue team in Nicaragua. She was trapped in mud flowing from the Casita volcano during Hurricane Mitch.

All told, Mitch took over 11 000 lives. It was the most deadly Atlantic hurricane since a 1780 storm that killed 22 000 in Barbados. President Carlos Flores of Honduras said Hurricane Mitch was "the worst disaster of the century."

# DISASTER DATA

Hurricane Mitch was the second deadliest Atlantic hurricane of the past 500 years. Here are the region's top eight killers. (Notice that only the most recent hurricanes have names.)

| Place | Year | # Killed |
|---|---|---|
| 1. Barbados, St. Eustatius and Martinique | 1780 | 22 000 |
| 2. Central America (Hurricane Mitch) | 1998 | 11 000 |
| 3. Galveston, Texas | 1900 | 8 000–12 000 |
| 4. Honduras (Hurricane Fifi) | 1974 | 8 000–10 000 |
| 5. Dominican Republic | 1930 | 2 000–8 000 |
| 6. Haiti and Cuba (Hurricane Flora) | 1963 | 8 000 |
| 7. Guadeloupe | 1776 | 6 000 |
| 8. Newfoundland | 1775 | 4 000 |

A young boy and his father clean up after the hurricane that terrorized Galveston, Texas, on September 8, 1900. Thousands of people were killed when the hurricane's giant storm surge flooded their homes without warning.

# Interview with a Hurricane Hunter

A NOAA (National Oceanic and Atmospheric Adminstration) plane flies over the circular eye of Hurricane Caroline in August 1975. Both NOAA and the United States Air Force Reserve crews regularly venture right into the center of tropical storms and fully formed hurricanes.

"Fly into a hurricane? You must be crazy!" That's often the response Christa Hornbaker gets when she tells people about her work as a hurricane hunter with the United States Air Force Reserve. In this interview, Christa explains why she ventures into some of the worst storms in the world.

**What made you interested in becoming a hurricane hunter?**

I've always been fascinated with weather. I studied weather at college and read lots of books, but this is better than they said in the books. This is the theory in action. Wow!

**What's the purpose of flying into hurricanes?**

We go into a storm and collect data for the National Hurricane Center in Miami. The data goes into computer models and improves their forecasting ability. We'll probably never get 100 percent accuracy, but I'm hoping to help people get out of the way.

**What do you do during a flight?**

I'm a mission director. I direct the pilot to find the center of the storm.

**How do you do that?**

Sensors on the airplane feed information about temperature, pressure, humidity and wind speed into a computer. It's constantly updated. I watch the data on the computer screen and decide if we should turn right or left to reach the eye of the storm.

## What's it like inside a hurricane?

Each storm has its own personality. Sometimes it's like a regular airplane ride, but things can get a little rough. Sometimes when you think it's going to be fairly smooth, you get into trouble, especially if the storm is changing.

## What's the scariest thing that's happened to you?

One time flying into Hurricane Georges, we started to get some hail. That's rare in tropical systems because the air is so warm. Hail can damage a plane, so we got pretty nervous. One of our oil coolers broke, and we had to shut down one engine. Luckily, we had three other engines and we got back safely, with just a few dents on the plane.

## Has anything else made you nervous?

We flew over Key West, Florida, on our way to Hurricane Georges. People knew the storm might hit Key West, but when I looked down from the plane, I noticed a lot of cars on the road. They didn't look like they were leaving. It was a beautiful day right there, but 645 km (400 mi.) away was a bad storm. That was scary. They were lucky Georges didn't get stronger — and that it didn't hit them directly.

A NOAA pilot checks his bearings while flying into a storm. Hurricane hunters collect valuable information that helps weather experts save lives by predicting a hurricane's track and intensity.

Computers and weather sensors help hurricane hunters set their course. Successful storm hunting depends on both technology and teamwork.

## ᘉᘉᘉ  ᘉᘉᘉ  You Try It  ᘉᘉᘉ  ᘉᘉᘉ

You can find out more about hurricane hunters at this Web site:
**www.omao.noaa.gov/aoc/aoc.html**

Take an imaginary flight into the eye of a hurricane by clicking on "Cyberflight into the Eye" at this Web site:
**www.hurricanehunters.com**

# STORM WARNING

Like an "eye in the sky," GOES I-M (a new Geostationary Operational Environmental Satellite) hovers 36 000 km (22 000 mi.) above Earth's surface. GOES satellites gather data that helps meteorologists keep a close watch on hurricanes.

No one can stop a hurricane. But with enough warning, people can get out of its way. Over the past twenty-five years, the National Hurricane Center in Miami, Florida, has improved the accuracy of its warnings and saved hundreds of lives.

The Hurricane Center uses new technology to help improve its forecasts. Meteorologists (weather scientists) gather information from weather satellites to analyze storm clouds. They also collect data from "hurricane hunter" planes that fly into hurricanes and drop sensors called dropsondes. These small devices take temperature, humidity, wind speed and wind direction readings. Barometers on the planes measure air pressure and help scientists locate the storm's center, where pressure readings are lowest.

Near the coast, hurricanes are monitored by land-based radar systems. Radar sensors bounce signals off raindrops, enabling scientists to study a hurricane's rain bands, track its path and predict where it is headed.

In 1938, a giant hurricane took northeastern United States by surprise. Because weather satellites did not yet exist, scientists had no way to track the hurricane's path. In this photo, rescue squads search for victims of the unexpected storm.

All the collected information is entered into computers and analyzed using a variety of programs that help meteorologists make their predictions.

In spite of all the new technological advances, hurricane forecasting isn't easy. A hurricane doesn't move predictably. It interacts with the ocean below and air around it in complex ways. A small change in the temperature or speed of a tropical storm can result in huge differences in its final path and intensity.

Frightened flamingoes huddle in a public washroom at the Miami Metrozoo on September 14, 1999. Zoo staff sheltered the birds indoors after warnings that Hurricane Floyd might strike the area.

In Cocoa Beach, Florida, residents boarded windows and evacuated the area after warnings from weather officials. As though obeying this shopkeeper's message, Hurricane Floyd turned northward and avoided Florida.

## You Try It

Weather forecasters use instruments called barometers to measure air pressure. You can build a simple barometer and track air pressure changes at home.

Expand a balloon by blowing it up and letting the air out. Cut off the neck of the balloon, and stretch the rest over the opening of a wide-mouthed jar. Hold the balloon in place with an elastic band. Now tape a straw to the stretched balloon so that it extends from one side of the jar. Place the jar near a wall, and

tape a piece of paper up beside it. Mark the position of the straw. Check your barometer every day and mark the level of the straw.

What do you notice about the weather when the straw is high? When it is low? Air pressing down on the balloon makes the straw point up. Higher air pressure usually brings clear weather. When the straw is low, air pressure is down. Lower air pressure often brings unsettled, cloudy weather.

# Dealing with DANGER

Weather experts are working toward more accurate predictions of when and where hurricanes will occur. But warnings are helpful only when people act wisely. With more and more people moving to coastal areas, knowing how to prepare for a hurricane is more important than ever.

FEMA (the U.S. Federal Emergency Management Agency) gives these pointers for people who live in or visit a hurricane-prone area.

• Know the risks in your area. Listen to radio and television weather news to keep up to date on current conditions. A hurricane "watch" means your area could be hit within thirty-six hours. A "warning" means that hurricane conditions are expected within twenty-four hours.

• Keep an emergency kit on hand. It should include a flashlight, a battery-operated radio, extra batteries, a first-aid kit, food and water supplies, essential medicines, sturdy shoes and a change of clothing.

**Dogs ride to safety in a boat towed by members of the FEMA Search and Rescue Team. The team saved dozens of stranded pets after Hurricane Floyd flooded the Tar River in North Carolina.**

• Prepare a family disaster plan. Choose a meeting place outside your neighborhood in case you become separated. Also, ask a friend or relative in another part of the country to be your family's contact, and make sure everyone knows this person's phone number. Plan several escape routes so that you know where to go if you need to leave quickly.

• When a hurricane watch or warning has been issued, bring in all outdoor objects, such as lawn furniture and garden tools, that might fly around and cause damage in high winds. Cover windows with plywood or wooden shutters.

• If an evacuation is ordered, leave as soon as possible. Remember to take your emergency kit with you!

Why wait for disaster to strike? Crews move a church out of harm's way in Tivoli, Pennsylvania. Hurricanes had flooded the building several times before the March 2001 relocation.

## DISASTER DATA

Can people control a hurricane? Probably not, but many have tried. Project Stormfury was one attempt. The idea was to scatter chemicals from planes. These chemicals would act as "seeds" for the formation of ice crystals and raindrops. As rain fell from the eye wall of the hurricane, the eye would expand and the hurricane's intensity would drop. Although Stormfury seemed to slow the winds of Hurricane Debbie in 1969, further flights had little success. Most scientists have now abandoned the idea of controlling hurricanes.

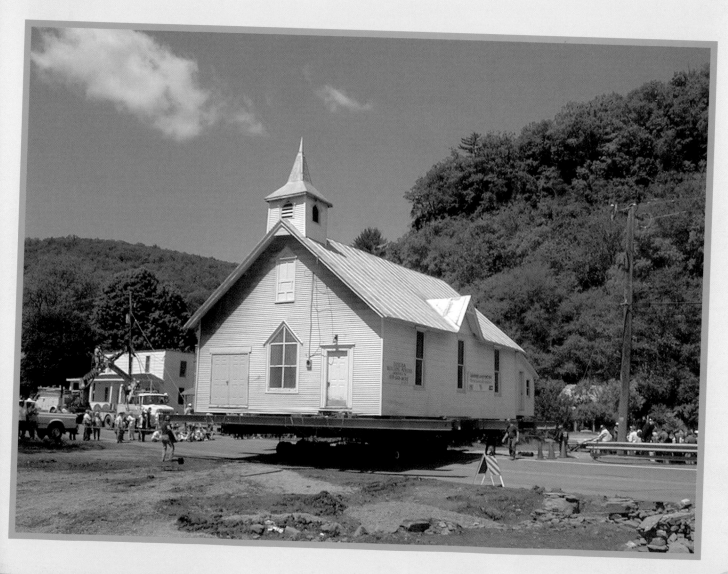

# Andrew Batters FLORIDA

In August 1992, a small tropical storm moved west across the Atlantic Ocean. For a time, it weakened and seemed about to disappear. Then, within two days, the storm intensified. On the morning of August 22, it roared to life as Hurricane Andrew.

Experts at the National Hurricane Center in Miami tracked Andrew closely. They predicted that the hurricane would soon hit the east coast of Florida. Orders were given to evacuate the coast. Over two million people left their homes and headed inland.

A rooftop sign explains the destruction in this Florida neighborhood. Hurricane Andrew killed 26 people directly. Another 39 died after the storm. Without the warnings of weather experts, many more people would have been killed.

Hurricane Andrew's winds picked up this board and drove it through the trunk of a palm tree in Homestead, Florida. The town was nearly flattened by Andrew's savage and powerful winds.

Hurricane Andrew reached land just after midnight on August 24. Its winds shrieked at over 280 km/h (175 m.p.h.). Houses crumpled. Trees twisted and broke. Cars were lifted into the air and flipped upside down. Worst hit were the towns of Homestead and Florida City.

Andrew missed the center of Miami by just 32 km (20 mi.). It struck the Miami Metrozoo, releasing monkeys and other wild animals from their enclosures. While most of the zoo's birds and mammals survived, their homes were ruined.

The devastation caused by Andrew was enormous. But it could have been even worse. In spite of its record-breaking destruction of property, Andrew's death toll was low compared to that of previous hurricanes of similar strength. The warnings of hurricane forecasters and prompt evacuation saved many lives.

Mobile homes are easy targets for a hurricane because they aren't anchored to the ground as permanent houses are. Residents of this trailer park were shocked by the damage caused by Hurricane Andrew's violent category 4 winds.

# Earth's
# BIGGEST STORMS

Hurricanes are powerful forces of nature. They help balance heat and moisture around the Earth. But when a hurricane strikes an area where people live, it can be disastrous.

As scientists learn more about hurricanes, they make better forecasts. Their warnings are quickly spread by radio, television and the Internet. As a result, in North America, the number of people killed by hurricanes has dropped. Still, property damage has risen as more people have moved to coastal areas. In other parts of the world, where housing and communications are poor, hurricanes continue to cause tremendous loss of life.

Many questions remain unanswered. Why do some storms suddenly change direction? Will global warming bring more hurricanes? In the future, scientists will continue to probe the mysteries of hurricanes, Earth's most powerful and deadly storms.

**Cracked pavement and a washed-out road remind North Carolina residents of Hurricane Floyd's visit.**

# Glossary

**Air pressure:** the pushing force of air weighing down on a particular place

**Barometer:** an instrument for measuring air pressure

**Cloud streets:** see Rain bands

**Cyclone:** the name used for a hurricane in the southwest Pacific and Indian oceans

**Dropsonde:** a weather-measuring device dropped into a hurricane from a plane

**Eye:** the clear, central portion of a hurricane

**Eye wall:** the band of clouds surrounding the eye of a hurricane

**Hurricane:** a vast, spinning storm with winds over 119 km/h (74 m.p.h.)

**Meteorologist:** a scientist who studies the weather

**Rain bands:** rows of clouds circling the center of a hurricane

**Saffir-Simpson scale:** a ranking of hurricane strength and destructiveness, from category 1 to category 5

**Storm surge:** a huge bulge of ocean water pushed up onto the shoreline by a hurricane

**Tornado:** a spinning wind funnel reaching down to the ground from a thunderstorm. Tornadoes sometimes form within hurricanes.

**Tropical storm:** a spinning storm with winds between 63 km/h (39 m.p.h.) and 118 km/h (73 m.p.h.). If conditions are right, tropical storms develop into hurricanes.

**Typhoon:** the name used for a hurricane in the China Sea

# Index